EAST LANCASHIRE RAILWAY
in colour

Gavin Morrison

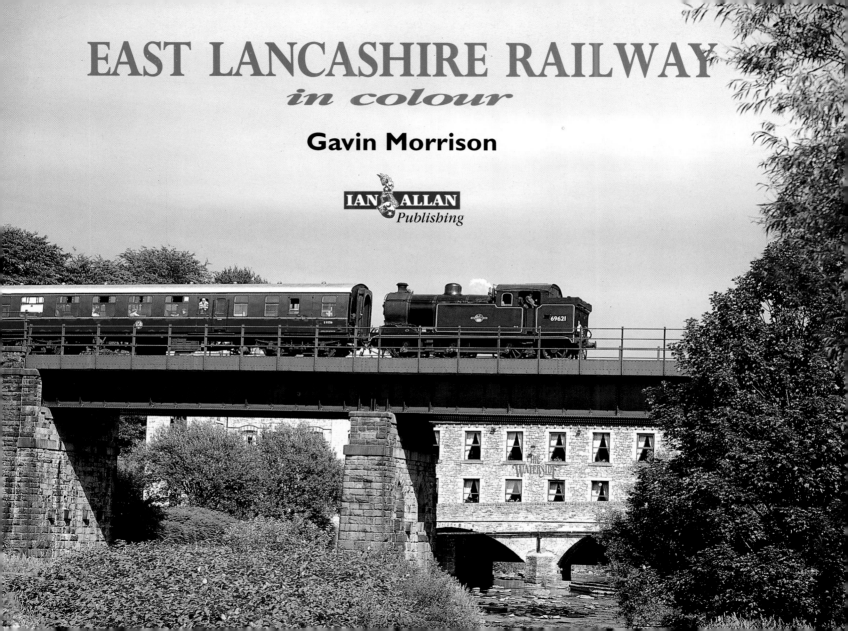

IAN ALLAN
Publishing

First published 1996

ISBN 0 7110 2466 9

© Ian Allan Ltd 1996

Published by Ian Allan Publishing

an imprint of Ian Allan Ltd, Terminal House, Station Approach, Shepperton, Surrey TW17 8AS. Printed by Ian Allan Printing Ltd, Coombelands House, Coombelands Lane, Addlestone, Surrey KT15 1HY.

Front cover: On 6 September 1995 Lancashire & Yorkshire 'A' class 0-6-0 No 52322 arrived at the railway from Steamtown, Carnforth, on permanent loan. Built at Horwich in January 1896 as No 1300 it became LMSR No 12322 and then BR No 52322 on Nationalisation. It was withdrawn from Lees shed (26E) in August 1962, having spent many years at Newton Heath and so, no doubt, it was a regular visitor to Rawtenstall and Bacup. It was purchased for preservation by Leonard Fairclough and sent to Horwich Works for restoration as No 1122. This identity was chosen by Mr Fairclough as he wanted a locomotive built during the year of his birth. No 52140 had been offered, but this was fitted with a Belpaire firebox and therefore not in original condition.

Apprentices restored the locomotive to a very high standard and it was delivered to Mr Fairclough's company at Adlington. During 1976 the locomotive was moved to Steamtown, where much cladding was replaced and boiler work done. By 1982 the locomotive was in steam for the first time since the early 1960s as L&YR No 1300 working the short Crag Bank shuttles. It was repainted again in 1993 to its BR livery. 1996 will see its centenary at Bury in L&YR livery as No 1300. It is seen at Burrs on 25 October 1995 with a special freight, run for a group of enthusiasts. *Tom Heavyside*

Back cover: Two of the diesel locomotives which have been at the railway for many years, Class 40 No D335 and Class 24 No D5054, make a splendid sight as they head through the cutting at Burrs *en route* to Bury on 6 October 1991. A brief history of the Class 40 appears in the caption on page 51. The Class 24 arrived in October 1983 from March depot, having been withdrawn in July 1976. Its last duty for BR was as a carriage heating unit at Cambridge. This combination of locomotives was photographed by the author in the early 1960s on the up 'Royal Scot' descending Shap, although on that occasion the Class 24 was the leading locomotive. *Author*

Title page: No 69621 is the only 'N7' in existence, out of a class of 134. It was the last engine to be built at Stratford Works in March 1924 by the LNER to a Great Eastern design. It was eventually withdrawn in September 1962 and, as its new owner lived near Leeds, it finished up being stored at Neville Hill shed for 11 years before moving to the East Anglian Railway Museum at Chappel & Wakes Colne station. A complete rebuild over many years followed, a process which was concluded in 1990. The locomotive arrived for a three-month visit to the line in May 1991 and is shown crossing Brooksbottom Viaduct heading for Bury. *David Dyson*

Left: Unrebuilt 'Battle of Britain' No 34072 *257 Squadron* arrived on the railway in October 1991 and, from the mileage chart published in the society's excellent magazine, managed to clock up 1,260 miles in 16 days' steaming by the end of the year. It also operated on several occasions in early 1992, and there are many photographs showing the magnificent exhausts that were produced. On 17 November 1991 it was putting up one of its spectacular performances in Burrs cutting on an atmospheric day. As there are no less than 20 'West Country'/'Battle of Britain' locomotives in preservation, it is surprising that one is not resident on the ELR. No 34072 is based on the Swanage Railway and was built at Brighton in April 1948. It was withdrawn in October 1964 from Eastleigh and sent to Barry for scrap in February 1965. It was later rescued and restored at Swindon. *Brian Dobbs*

Introduction

The history of the East Lancashire Railway Preservation Society is one of great courage and determination by a very small but dedicated band of enthusiasts, against enormous difficulties, over many years, whereby they ultimately finished up preserving a different stretch of line to that originally intended.

Unlike some of the other preserved lines, the ELRPS entered the field very late; more than 20 years from the date of withdrawal of passenger services by BR to the reopening specials, but the speed with which the line has developed and expanded cannot really be matched by any other railway preservation scheme in the country.

The original group was named the Helmshore & District Railway Preservation Society, whose aim was to preserve the section of line from Stubbins Junction to Accrington. Closure of the line was announced in September 1966, after it had been in operation for 120 years. A meeting took place on 25 November 1966 and the society was formed, with eight council members. This appeared to be a good start.

Little progress was made in the first 12 months and members started to vanish as rumours circulated that Haslingden Corporation was going to purchase part of the trackbed and remove a bridge. A meeting was called to abandon the project, but five members voted to try and save the line from Stubbins Junction to Helmshore, a distance of some 3.5 miles. The station at Helmshore was leased from BR for one year and fund-raising activities commenced. In 1968 there were 120 members and £150 in the kitty. To put things into perspective, BR wanted £40,000 for the track and £600 for the land with an immediate 10% deposit. By now Haslingden Corporation had turned against the society, but even so an Open Day was held attracting 1,619 people.

The first stock arrived in 1969, followed by steam and diesel locomotives in mid-1970. Another Gala Day was held drawing 3,500 with Class 5 No 44806 in steam. BR started lifting the track in 1971 and eventually it was agreed that by all that there was no future at Helmshore and a new site was required. Many possibilities were considered around Lancashire, but eventually the former East Lancashire Railway warehouse at Castlecroft, Bury, was selected and a one-year lease negotiated with Bury Council. Locomotives and stock were moved from Helmshore in May 1972 and the site became known as the Bury Transport Museum, offering space to both road and rail vehicles. The museum was opened by the mayor on 26 August 1972. During this time the last passenger train had run between Bury and Rawtenstall and BR made it clear that its track was not available for the operation of preserved rolling stock. More items of stock continued to arrive, but it was a long wait until 1980 before the society saw any hope of running trains.

The electric trains from Bury to Manchester moved to a new station in Bury in March 1980 and the connection to that line was severed at Loco Junction. A right-angled cross-over was installed just outside the new interchange to allow the two coal trains per week to continue running to Rawtenstall. After all this it came as a surprise when BR announced that coal traffic was to cease in December 1980. A final DMU 'farewell' special was operated. Despite the passing of 12 years, the society was, however, still short of money.

Reproduced by kind permission of Martin Bairstow and John Holroyd.

3

The real turning point came on 19 March 1981 when the society met representatives of BR and Greater Manchester, Lancashire, Bury and Rossendale councils. The object was to persuade the councils that a light railway would be beneficial to the area. The attitude from the councils was very different from that of 10 years earlier and BR agreed to postpone lifting the track.

A decision was taken to run a charter train on 27 March 1982, the cost being guaranteed by Greater Manchester. This was a great success and no financial loss resulted. Three trains were run, carrying 1,300 passengers, including representatives of the interested councils, and some 2,000 visited the museum.

Relations with the councils continued to be good and more rolling stock arrived. The key factor in the future of the railway was the derelict land grant, whereby Greater Manchester and Rossendale could recover £1.2 million of the anticipated £1.7 million cost of reclaiming and developing the land surrounding the railway up the valley. The outcome was that the councils purchased the land from BR and leased it to the East Lancashire Railway Trust for 90 years. The trust then subleased the line to the railway company. The line was in a very poor state, sections of the line had been virtually demolished and four bridges needed replacement. Several optimistic forecasts were given for the reopening and more stock continued to arrive. Greater Manchester Council applied for a light railway order early in 1985, but it was abolished in March 1986, and its functions taken over by the Metropolitan Borough of Bury, who supported the whole project.

British Rail banned all movement of preserved stock on the line, unlike other preservation movements that had been allowed to run works trains, but on 27 December 1986 the first works train ran to Summerseat. From then on the rate of progress was unbelievable, and the opening train ran to Ramsbottom on 25 July 1987.

On 31 May 1988 the first works train reached Irwell Vale, but it was not until 5 November 1989 before a similar train arrived at Rawtenstall. The extension reopened to passengers on 27 April 1991, the ultimate reward to the few who had battled away against all the odds for 20 years.

The captions to the photographs cover most of the relevant events and developments up to 1996, but what of the future?

The future as seen in 1996 can really be covered under four different headings: 1, Buckley Wells; 2, Heywood Extension; 3, Castlecroft Museum; 4, Development of Traffic.

Buckley Wells depot is a listed building, as it was part of the original East Lancashire Railway Works built in 1852. It is on a 21-acre site, and is a 5-road shed. The building has been repaired and is in reasonable condition, and houses many of the line's locomotives as well as Ian Riley's Engineering Company (he is also the chief engineer to the railway). Locomotives from other societies are repaired as well as those from the ELR. The local authority owns the site and it is the intention to develop it as a railway centre and landscape the area.

The Heywood Extension trackbed is owned by the East Lancashire Trust and the track by the railway. The line was purchased from BR with assistance from the European Regional Developer Fund. The track is currently in a fit state to run trains; in fact stock has arrived and departed this way, but before services can start there is a lot of resignalling work to be carried out around Bury South and Bolton Street. There is also the need to sort out a satisfactory working at Green Lane level crossing. The current hopes are that services may start in the summer of 1997.

The lease on the Bury Transport Museum expires in 1997. Recent developments have involved discussions with the Museum of Transport, Manchester, who want extra space. It would appear there is a great opportunity for the benefit of both groups to have a joint operation. It is intended that Castlecroft will continue to be known as Bury Transport Museum.

Finally there is the question of running a commuter service up the valley, occasional specials starting from Bury, and even freight connecting with Railtrack. It is known the local councils are quite in favour of commuter services, probably using DMUs, and that it is something that would assist the road congestion in the area. What really has to be sorted out is how to retain the atmosphere, and period styling, and run a modern commuter service at the same time. The railway is probably better placed than most other preserved lines for such a service, but we will have to wait and see how things develop.

Much of the information given in the introduction and captions has been obtained from the excellent publication by Martin Bairstow, 'The East Lancashire Railway', and it is thoroughly recommended to readers who wish to learn more of the line's history.

I am extremely grateful to the photographers who have so willingly offered their excellent work for publication. I have tried to show as many different locomotives as possible that have worked on the line, but with only 70 pictures there are some omissions. My thanks to several fellow members for information about the locomotives, and especially to Publicity Director Graham Vevers for his help.

Below: It is very likely that 'Princess Coronation' No 46225 *Duchess of Gloucester* stood alongside No 71000 *Duke of Gloucester* on Crewe North shed during BR days. This fine picture was taken at Bury Buckley Wells in August 1994, and as is frequently the case with many pictures on the line, all is not what it seems. Visiting 'Princess Coronation' No 6233 *Duchess of Sutherland* had smoke deflectors added in addition to a repaint and a renumbering. The locomotive is in need of major repairs before it can be steamed, but was recently sold by Bressingham and has been moved to Butterley. *Duke of Gloucester* is now based at Buckley Wells when it is not busy on main line duties. The history of No 71000 requires a book in itself, but its restoration must be regarded as probably the major achievement in the locomotive preservation movement. Not only is it restored to its former glory, but it is now a vastly superior locomotive to what it was when in BR service. *Brian Dobbs*

Far left: A view taken from the top of Bolton Street Tunnel on 9 August 1963 presents a very different picture from today. Newton Heath 'Jubilee' No 45661 *Vernon* heads the 5.10pm Nelson-Moston vans service. In the distance can be seen Tottington Junction signalbox; notice the left-hand line is electrified. On the right are School Brow coal sidings, whilst on the left are the disused Castlecroft Sidings, where the Bury Transport Museum has been situated since 1972 in the former goods warehouse. *Eric Bentley*

Left: An interesting picture at Summerseat shows Newton Heath-based Class 5 No 44735 leaving on a Saturday half-day excursion to Southport. Notice the sidings on the right which have long since gone. In the background can be seen a diesel multiple-unit working the 12.5pm Bury Bolton Street-Bacup service. Goods traffic ceased at Summerseat on 28 December 1964, whilst the passenger service survived until 3 June 1972. *Eric Bentley*

Above: Taken shortly before the service finished on 3 June 1972, a dirty Class 105 DMU, in plain blue livery, crosses Brooksbottom Viaduct. The church on the left with the corrugated iron roof has now been demolished. The chimney in the background belonged to the old Joshua Hoyles Mill, which has now been converted into flats. *David Mills*

Left: The 5.10pm Nelson-Moston van train, 5J13, is seen from above the northern entrance of Nuttal Tunnel, headed by Newton Heath 'Jubilee' No 45642 *Boscawen*. This locomotive was the original 'Jubilee' No 5552 *Silver Jubilee*, exchanging identities in April 1935. The new No 5552 was painted in a special glossy black livery embellished with chromium fittings. This was carried out because the locomotive was the newest 'Jubilee' to be completed prior to the Silver Jubilee of King George V, when the locomotive was exhibited at Euston. Sixty years later preserved 'Jubilee' No 45593 *Kolhapur* was repainted in this special livery and ran on the ELR. At least 12 mill chimneys can be seen in this photograph taken on 1 July 1964. *Eric Bentley*

Left: The 'B7' code at the head of the Class 105 Cravens-built DMU indicates that the six-car set entering Ramsbottom was heading for either Colne or Skipton. The code 'B2' was used for the Bacup trains. The picture was taken in July 1966. The DMUs on these services were introduced from the summer of 1954 onwards and in early 1956 Bury shed took delivery of seven twin-car Metro-Cammell sets. A half-hour service to Bacup was operated, with an hourly one to Accrington and beyond. *David Mills*

Right: The driver and the shunter have a chat before starting to sort out the wagons at Rawtenstall in July 1972. At that time this train ran daily, and on this occasion Class 25 No 5155 was in charge. This locomotive was built at Darlington in 1961, becoming No 25005 under the TOPS scheme and was withdrawn in December 1980, which curiously was the same month that the coal trains ceased to run to Rawtenstall; Friday the fifth was the last day of operation north of Bury. *David Mills*

Above: A view taken from Belle Vue Terrace footbridge on 4 July 1979 shows a Class 504 EMU in plain blue livery leaving Bury for Manchester Victoria. Bury South signalbox is in the background. The Manchester-Bury line was closed by British Railways in 1991 and was converted into the Light Rapid Transit system (Manchester Metrolink), which opened on 6 April 1992. This section of line was used to provide a connection from the ELR to BR, but this is now achieved by the Heywood extension. Opened in 1879, the line was electrified back in 1916. The Class 504 EMUs were built in 1959 for the 9¾-mile journey to Manchester. Originally they were painted green, then plain blue, and blue and grey, before finally emerging in the Greater Manchester PTE livery of orange and brown as illustrated on page 22. *Tom Heavyside*

Above: A wintry scene taken at Bury Bolton Street on 30 December 1979 shows a two-car Class 504 unit headed by No 77176 in the bay with another set ready to depart to Manchester. This picture makes an interesting comparison with the picture taken 12 years later shown on page 17. The last electric train departed from Bury Bolton Street on Friday 14 March 1980, and the tracks were realigned over the following weekend so that the trains could be operated from the new Interchange. This work created a right-angled crossing on the site of the former Bury Knowsley Street station with the original line through Bolton Street used solely by the coal trains from Castleton to Rawtenstall. *Tom Heavyside*

Left: The last train from Rawtenstall, the 'Rawtenstall Farewell', was a six-car DMU which ran on 14 February 1981 and carried 300 passengers. It ran from Manchester Victoria to Rawtenstall via Heywood and Bury, calling at Bolton Street on the outward journey to allow passengers to visit the Bury Transport Museum. The special is seen rounding the sharp curve between Bolton Street and Knowsley Street, with Bury South signalbox in the background. It is headed by a Cravens Class 105 unit; 25 of these units were allocated in March 1961 to work services in East Lancashire. They were powered by Rolls-Royce 238hp engines and fitted with hydraulic transmission. Note the amount of undergrowth surrounding the line which has now been cleared, and the Rawtenstall station nameboard in the cab window. *Tom Heavyside*

Right: The original East Lancashire Railway opened in 1846 and became part of the Lancashire & Yorkshire Railway in 1857. The new ELR appeared in 1987, but prior to that date the small but dedicated band of enthusiasts had had a very difficult 10 years. The preservation group was originally the Helmshore & District Society, which aimed to preserve the 3½-mile route from Stubbins Junction to Haslingden. At first things went well with promise of support from Haslingden Corporation, but progress was slow and interest waned. The little Andrew Barclay 0-4-0ST from the North West Gas Board, built in 1927, was the first steam locomotive to arrive in August 1970. Eventually the project was abandoned and a new site was found at the former ELR warehouse at Castlecroft, Bury. The stock was moved from Helmshore in May 1972, and so the Bury Transport Museum emerged. The 0-4-0 ST is seen shunting in the yard on 31 July 1977. This locomotive was the first to reach Ramsbottom, in 1987, and Rawtenstall in November 1989. *Tom Heavyside*

Above: Another milestone in the history of the railway was 27 April 1991 when the first passenger train ran through to Rawtenstall. The locomotives were the same as those used on the opening special to Ramsbottom back on 25 July 1987 — No 32 *Gothenburg*, built by Hudswell-Clarke in 1903 for the Manchester Ship Canal Co, pilots Robert Stephenson & Hawthorn 0-6-0T No 1, which was built in 1950. The latter was loaned to the East Somerset Railway in 1991/92 but was stored on its return awaiting firebox repairs.
Mike Taylor

Above: Flying Scotsman is without doubt the most famous locomotive in the world and is by far the most widely travelled on the British Railways network, not to mention its travels in the USA in 1970 and, more recently, Australia. It visited the ELR during February and March 1993 and is shown at Bury Bolton Street waiting to leave for Rawtenstall. The history of the locomotive has been recorded many times, but it is a thought that the locomotive has been in preservation for 33 years, only eight years less than its working life with the LNER and BR, and it has been in working order for virtually all its career of 74 years. It had been in LNER livery whilst running over BR lines, but during the last few years it has returned to the BR livery with German-style smoke deflectors and double chimney. These features were originally installed at Doncaster Works in 1959. It is currently awaiting a major overhaul at Slough. *David Dyson*

Left: Rebuilt 'Merchant Navy' No 35005 *Canadian Pacific* made a short two-week visit from the Great Central Railway in 1991. It is shown in Bolton Street after arriving with the 18.00 service from Rawtenstall on 3 August, and is carrying the 'Atlantic Coast Express' headboard. The bay platform on the left is full of coaching stock and a couple of Class 25 diesels. This picture makes an interesting comparison with the one taken 12 years earlier on page 12.
Tom Heavyside

PLATFORM
3

Above: A lovely night shot at Bury Bolton Street with disguised LMS '4F' No 4422 on loan from Cheddleton about to leave with a demonstration freight train on 3 December 1992. No 44311 was allocated to the 26 (Manchester) Area, being at Newton Heath in the autumn of 1961 and possibly Bolton later on. No 4422 was a Somerset & Dorset locomotive for many years and so, in recent years, it has been used during S&D weekends by several preserved lines. Built in 1927, No 4422 worked until 1965 when it was sent to the Barry scrapyard of Woodham Bros from where it was bought in 1977 and restored by the North Staffordshire Railway.
Brian Dobbs

Left: **Duchess of Sutherland** visited the railway in 1993 from Bressingham and it was not surprising that the opportunity was taken to disguise it as other members of the class. It was one of the batch of five built in 1938 at Crewe without streamline casing. It went to Camden shed until 1944 and it was then transferred to Crewe, where it remained until 1960. It was then transferred to Edge Hill, Liverpool, being the only member of the class to be allocated to that shed at any time. Withdrawal came on 8 February 1964 and, along with a number of other locomotives, was bought by Butlins Ltd and restored externally almost to its original condition. It then spent 10 years at the Heads of Ayr holiday camp before being transferred to Bressingham, where it remained until recently. During the trip to the ELR it came as no surprise that it appeared as No 46246 *City of Manchester.* The locomotive is shown in Bolton Street on 14 September 1993. *Brian Dobbs*

Right: One could be forgiven for thinking this superb line-up was taken at the Great Western Society's centre at Didcot rather than at the North shed in Bury on the evening of Friday 13 November 1992. The locomotives were being prepared for the railway's first Great Western Weekend. Restored 'Manor' No 7828 *Odney Manor* is on the left; it is in BR green livery with an 84J Croes Newydd shed plate. Next is No 5029 *Nunney Castle* from Didcot, sporting the 'Cornishman' headboard in GWR livery. Finally, heavy freight 2-8-0T No 5224 in BR black livery completes the trio. Note the 38F shed code, which is presumably to indicate Loughborough on the preserved Great Central as the code was not used by BR. *Mike Taylor*

Above: A very busy scene at Bury North shed shows a wide variety of motive power. On the left is visiting Great Eastern 'N7' No 69621 (disguised as No 69614); alongside and just visible is 'Manor' No 7828 *Odney Manor* (built in December 1950 and withdrawn in October 1965). Rebuilt 'Merchant Navy' No 35005 *Canadian Pacific* was built, as No 21C5, in 1941, rebuilt in May 1959 and withdrawn in October 1965. On the right is Derek Foster's Standard 2-6-0 No 76079, although on this occasion the smokebox numberplate shows No 76031 and the cabside No 76039! The locomotives were in steam for a big engine weekend on 2 August 1991. *Tom Heavyside*

Above: With some locomotives facing north and others south on the railway, occasionally rather odd double-headed sights appear. Looking superb in its BR blue livery, which it carried between September 1950 and April 1952, No 60007 *Sir Nigel Gresley* pilots resident Class 5 No 5407 towards Bury just south of Burrs on 29 October 1995 with the 14.00 service from Rawtenstall. The corridor tender is shown to advantage. The 'A4' was withdrawn in February 1966, purchased for preservation and taken to Crewe Works in July the same year. It was out running trial trips in March 1967 and then put up some terrific performances on enthusiast specials until steam was banned on the main line in 1968. It re-emerged in 1972 on the main line and has continued to do so ever since. The locomotive achieved 112mph descending Stoke Bank in 1959 on a Stephenson Locomotive Society special with its regular driver, the legendary Bill Hoole of King's Cross shed, at the regulator. Most of its working life was spent based at King's Cross (Top Shed) and Grantham sheds, but it completed its BR life on the three-hour Glasgow-Aberdeen expresses based at Aberdeen Ferryhill. *Tom Heavyside*

Above: What must be a unique combination in British railway preservation occurred during the autumn Diesel Gala in 1991. Two of the ex-BR Class 504 two-car EMU sets, Nos M65461 +M77182 and M65451+M77172, were adapted to run with Class 25 No 25262 in the centre. The units were still in the Greater Manchester PTE livery. This fascinating combination is seen just south of Burrs heading for Bury on 6 October 1991. This scene can never be repeated since a decision was made to scrap one of the two-car units because of the space it took up. This decision was taken after it had been offered free to any interested party; unfortunately, nobody wanted it. *Author*

Right: Photographed on 14 August 1994, No 7029 *Clun Castle* heads the 08.15 demonstration freight from Bury up the valley towards Burrs during its visit to the railway in the late summer of that year. 'Castle' class locomotives working freight trains on BR in the early 1960s were not unusual, but their external condition, normally without nameplates, was very different from the condition of No 7029 on this occasion. *Clun Castle* was one of the few locomotives to be in full working order when it entered preservation in early 1966 and it worked a number of specials before the end of main line steam, of which the most famous were over the East Coast main line to Newcastle, over Shap and the Settle-Carlisle line in 1967 after special clearance trials. Since the early 1970s it has been in regular use on the main line as well as visiting many preserved railways. *Brian Dobbs*

Above: Class 25s Nos 25262 and D7659 (the latter being renumbered 25309 and later 25909 in BR service) show the contrasting liveries in which the class was painted during BR service. The train is approaching Burrs *en route* to Rawtenstall on 6 June 1993. No 25262 was originally No D7612 when it emerged from Derby Works in April 1966 and entered service based in Glasgow. It was withdrawn in March 1987 numbered 25901. No D7659 was a product of Beyer-Peacock and entered traffic in July 1966 based on the London Midland Region; it survived until September 1985. No 25262 is currently under repair and is privately owned by a member of the society; it was originally preserved by Harry Needle, who obtained it from MC Metals in Glasgow after it had been stored at Carlisle. No D7659 is one of the locomotives owned by Pete Waterman.

Author

Right: During 1993 the railway was visited by two of the famous GWR 2-8-0s: No 3822 from Didcot and No 2857 from the Severn Valley Railway. This class must be one of the most successful type of freight locomotive ever to run in this country and it is remarkable that whilst No 2857 was built in May 1918, No 3822 did not arrive in stock until April 1940, during which period there were very few changes to the design. Few classes anywhere in the world were built with minimal alterations over a 39-year period. During the ELR's summer festival, on 17 August 1993, it was decided to try and set a haulage record for a passenger train on a preserved line. A remarkable 23-coach train was assembled and the locomotive blasted its way up the valley to Rawtenstall without much effort. Unfortunately the spectacular exhaust, as illustrated, was not appreciated by the local residents as apparently it continued all the way to Rawtenstall. The train is seen at Burrs at 18.30; the last three coaches are out of sight. *Mike Taylor*

Right: The ELR's diesel galas often produce some unlikely locomotive combinations. On 16 June 1995, due to some unscheduled alterations to the diagrams, one of the afternoon trains to Bury had the unusual pairing of Class 20 No 20042 and Class 50 No 50015, with Class 31 No D5518 (ex-No 31101) at the rear. The ensemble is pictured passing through the cutting at Burrs. No 20042 looks very smart in the black livery adopted by Pete Waterman, whilst No 50015 was in green undercoat as there was not time to repaint it before the gala, and the Class 31 was running in its original BR green livery for the first time. No 20042 entered service allocated to Norwich in November 1959 and was withdrawn in June 1991 from Thornaby. No 50015 was built in April 1968 at the Vulcan Foundry and was withdrawn from Laira in May 1992; it was the only member of the class ever to be painted in departmental livery. No D5518 went into service from Stratford in London during April 1958 and was withdrawn from Bescot in January 1993; it was the only representative of its class to receive the 'large logo' livery. *Author*

Left: David Shepherd's 2-10-0 No 92203 *Black Prince* was a very welcome visitor to the line. Normally based on the East Somerset Railway, it is one of a class of 251 '9F' locomotives built until March 1960, when BR's last new steam locomotive (No 92220 *Evening Star*) was completed. No 92203 was originally allocated to St Philip's Marsh, Bristol, in April 1959; it was withdrawn from Birkenhead in November 1967. Records exist of the class attaining 90mph down Stoke Bank and on the Great Central main line, and No 92203 is believed to hold a record for a British steam locomotive when it hauled a 2,178-ton train over lines in a quarry on 11 September 1982. It is shown working an early morning charter train in late 1995 at Burrs. There are nine '9Fs' in

preservation, one of which (No 92207) is under restoration at Bury. No 92203 was scheduled to leave the ELR in February 1996. *David Dyson*

Above: Looking north through the cutting at Burrs on 16 June 1995, Pete Waterman's Class 20 No 20188, in its smart black livery, heads an evening train towards Bury. An English Electric Vulcan Foundry-built locomotive dating from January 1967, No 20188 went to work for the Midland Division of the LMR and was withdrawn from Toton in January 1990. It was rescued from MC Metals in Glasgow for preservation. At the rear of the train is another Vulcan Foundry product, 'Deltic' No D9019. *Author*

Above: A sight to gladden the heart of any GWR enthusiast: then resident 'Manor' No 7828 *Odney Manor* pilots visiting 'Castle' No 7029 *Clun Castle* (from the Birmingham Railway Museum) *en route* to Ramsbottom through the cutting at Burrs. Neither locomotive was actually built by the GWR, but by BR after 1948 at Swindon. No 7029 entered service in May 1950 attached to a high-sided Hawksworth tender, whilst No 7828 emerged from the works in December the same year.

No 7029 was withdrawn in December 1965 with around 625,000 miles of service, a low figure for a 'Castle' averaging only 40,000 miles a year during its short life. It was in good working order when withdrawn and went into preservation immediately, since when it has been used on the main line many times. The double chimney was fitted in October 1959. It spent many years when new allocated to Newton Abbot. No 7828 was initially allocated to Neath and so it is doubtful if it ever piloted No 7029 over the Devon banks. Probably the nearest that either class would have got to the ELR in BR days was Chester, although No 7029 did traverse the Settle & Carlisle route in 1967. *Tom Heavyside*

Above: The railway has been fortunate in having many of Pete Waterman's fleet of diesels visiting it for gala events in addition to those based on the line. This picture shows Class 47 No 47402 shortly after it had arrived on the ELR piloting Class 50 No 50015 *Valiant*. The train is passing through the cutting at Burrs *en route* to Bury on 6 June 1993. The Class 47 entered service as No D1501 on 13 November 1962 and spent most of its life working the East Coast main line whilst allocated to Finsbury Park and Gateshead, although it was also frequently seen on trans-Pennine services. It was the locomotive involved in the fatal accident at Farnley Junction on 5 September 1977, when it hit a DMU killing both drivers. It finished its career at Immingham, from where it was withdrawn. It is now numbered 1501. No 50015 is currently being repainted at Bury. *Author*

Right: Although this delightful picture is undated, it was probably taken around 1990, before No 32 *Gothenburg* was repainted in blue as 'Thomas the Tank Engine'. This Hudswell-Clarke 0-6-0T, built in 1903 for the Manchester Ship Canal Co, has become one of the line's best-known locomotives amongst the general public since it arrived on the line in 1972. It is the main attraction at the very popular 'Thomas' weekends at Bury as well as elsewhere. It is shown leaving Summerseat on one of its infrequent outings up the valley. *David Dyson*

Above: The London & South Western Railway and the Southern built a fine selection of handsome 4-6-0s. One of these classes was the Urie-designed 'S15', of which 20 were built between March 1920 and May 1921, and were effectively the goods/mixed traffic version of the famous 'King Arthur' class. No 506 became BR No 30506; it entered traffic in October 1920, had a Maunsell superheater added in February 1930 and survived until January 1964. In this picture the locomotive is approaching Brooksbottom Viaduct after leaving Summerseat station on 26 August 1993. The locomotive was on the railway for about a month during the summer of 1993 on loan from the Mid-Hants Railway. Records show that the locomotive covered 1,227,897 miles in service. During their period of operation the appearance of these locomotives changed, with the addition of smoke deflectors and the replacement of the Urie chimney by one designed by Maunsell. *Mike Taylor*

Right: This unusual and spectacular view was taken from the 128ft high Peel monument on Holcombe Hill and shows the superb surrounding scenery, with Betty Beet's red-liveried Ivatt 2-6-0 No 46441 piloting Paddy Smith's Stanier Class 5 No 5407. The pair are seen crossing Brooksbottom Viaduct at Summerseat *en route* to Rawtenstall on 26 February 1995. The little Ivatt 2-6-0 has travelled extensively on main line duties in recent years.
Mike Taylor

Above: Stanier 'Jubilee' No 45593 *Kolhapur* arrived at the railway disguised as No 5552 *Silver Jubilee* in black livery with chrome embellishments. Whenever possible the ELR management takes the opportunity to run locomotives in different liveries. It was proposed that the Fowler tender from resident 'Crab' 2-6-0 No 42765 be attached and the locomotive painted in lined BR black livery. Looking very smart in this livery, *Kolhapur* is pictured crossing

Brooksbottom Viaduct as No 45698 *Mars*, which was one of the trio of 'Jubilees' based at Liverpool Bank Hall for many years and which were regular performers in the area. All three ran with Fowler tenders, although No 45719 *Glorious* had one of the 10 high-sided versions. All eventually received Stanier tenders. No 45593 was also disguised as No 45700 *Amethyst*, which was a Manchester Newton Heath locomotive.
Brian Dobbs

Right: Another 'first' for the line was on 5 November 1990 when the 13.00 from Bury was double-headed by ex-BR main line locomotives to Ramsbottom. Standard Class 4MT 4-6-0 No 75078 was visiting from the neighbouring Worth Valley line and was paired up with the then resident Standard 2-6-0 No 76079. There are six of the '4MT' 4-6-0s in preservation, two of them passed for main line running. No 75078 was built at Swindon in 1957 and spent most of its working life at Basingstoke, being withdrawn in 1966. It then spent the next six years at Barry before being rescued by the Standard Class 4 Preservation Society and moved to Keighley in June 1972. Ironically it was the intention of this group to preserve a 2-6-0 '4MT' from Barry (possibly No 76079), but the 4-6-0 was in better condition.

No 76079 was built in 1957 at Horwich and allocated to Sutton Oak. It was withdrawn nine years later and rescued from Barry in 1974, initially moving to Steamport (Southport). In 1982 it was purchased by Derek Foster and restored to working condition. It entered service on the ELR in August 1989. The pair make a superb sight on Brooksbottom Viaduct before entering the 423yd-long tunnel. *Mike Taylor*

Above: No 71000 *Duke of Gloucester* was built as a one-off and entered service on 18 May 1954, but with the dieselisation of the West Coast main line the locomotive never really had the chance to prove itself. There was also a reluctance amongst the drivers, who were wedded to the Stanier Pacifics, to operate it. After only 300,000 miles of service it was withdrawn on 24 November 1962. It languished at Crewe Works until early 1967. It was then decided that the valve gear and left-hand cylinder would be saved and the rest sold to Woodham Bros for scrap. In October No 71000 was sent to J. Cashmores in error, who after removing some parts sent it on to Woodhams.

Over six years later it was purchased for preservation, with the tender taken from '9F' No 92134. It moved to the Great Central Railway where the long process of restoration started. Many parts had to be made, some of which are not to the original specification, but on 25 May 1986 it made its first run. It then returned to Crewe Works to have its worn tyres replaced prior to moving to Didcot. Since 1990 it has worked main line specials, giving performances far in excess of anything achieved in its days with BR. It is shown in this picture crossing Brooksbottom Viaduct on 26 March 1994 with the 10.00 service from Bury to Rawtenstall. *Tom Heavyside*

Right: Class 24 No 24081 was on loan to the ELR in 1989 from the Steamport Railway Museum in Southport. Looking immaculate in BR blue livery, it is emerging from the north end of Brooksbottom Tunnel on the diesel gala weekend of 18 June that year, working the 11.00 from Bury to Ramsbottom. Built at Crewe, the locomotive entered traffic in March 1960 allocated to March shed, before becoming the last of the class to be withdrawn in October 1980. *Mike Taylor*

Above: No D1041 *Western Prince* was among the last batch of Class 52 diesel-hydraulics to be withdrawn by BR in February 1977. It was built at Crewe in October 1962. Most of the class lasted less than 14 years with BR and, on withdrawal, No D1041 was purchased by Tim Hanson. Initially it was based at Horwich Works before arriving at Bury on 11 February 1981. It makes a fine sight in this picture as it approaches Brooksbottom Tunnel *en route* to Rawtenstall. Considered by many to be the best looking of all the BR diesel fleet, this member of the class has been in maroon livery for several years and is pictured here, on 15 June 1991. *Author*

Above: The first services of the day during the diesel galas are often diagrammed for the line's DMUs. During the summer gala of 1992, the Class 110 'Calder Valley' unit was in operation. It is shown on 6 June ready to depart from Ramsbottom with the second train of the day to Rawtenstall. The two-car unit was formed of Nos E51813 and E51842; the trailer car No 59701 was then under restoration. The unit is now running in the original green livery. In the background is the battery-electric multiple-unit, Nos Sc79998 and Sc79999, which was later to become test unit *Gemini*. The original Ramsbottom station buildings were demolished in January 1971, having become unstaffed in March 1968. The rebuilt station was opened in 1989; the buildings came from a variety of sites — the shelter on the southbound platform, for example, coming from Daisy Hill near Wigan and the footbridge from Dinting. *Author*

Left: In the latter years of operation on the branch, the signalbox at Ramsbottom was reduced in status so that it just controlled the level crossing. Once passenger services were withdrawn, the coal trains took a travelling porter to open and shut the gates. The box has now been re-equipped to a high standard and has both manual and electronic interlocking. *Western Prince* is seen arriving from Rawtenstall on 15 June 1991. *Tom Heavyside*

Left: Class 4F No 4422 was built at Crewe in 1927 and finished its pre-preservation days at Barry, from where it was rescued in 1977. It was restored to working order by a dedicated group at Cheddleton on the North Staffordshire Railway. The ELR used to see visits by members of the class and No 4422 is shown at Ramsbottom station specially renumbered as No 44525 on 25 April 1993 when working an early morning photographers' special. The picture shows the restored water tank, signals, footbridge and level crossing, all of which have been returned to a 1950s appearance. It also shows that the sun does not always shine in the Irwell Valley, just in case the other photographs in this book give you that impression. *Mike Taylor*

Above: Class S160 2-8-0 No 5820 was built in 1945 for the US Army. It worked on the Polish State Railways from whom it was bought by members of the Keighley & Worth Valley Railway in 1977. Nicknamed 'Big Jim', it visited the ELR for just over a year between February 1992 and March 1993. In its distinctive grey livery, it is seen at Irwell Vale on 14 March 1992, on what appears to be a very cold day with snow on the surrounding hills. It is working the 12.00 from Bury. The ELR itself now possesses an 'S160', albeit in many pieces inside Buckley Wells shed. *Tom Heavyside*

Left: When *Sir Nigel Gresley* first visited the line in April and May 1994, it was running in its LNER blue livery that it carried in preservation from 1967 until late 1994. It was then repainted into the very attractive, but short-lived, BR lined blue livery as No 60007. It is shown at Irwell Vale with the 11.00 Bury-Rawtenstall train on 1 May 1994. Further details about the locomotive can be found in the caption for page 21. No 60007 is now based at Buckley Wells when not on main line duty. *Brian Dobbs*

Left: Currently the only working 'Crab' in the country, No 42765 was one of the 245 Hughes 2-6-0s modified by Henry Fowler. It was built at Crewe in 1927, as No 13065, and allocated to Kentish Town (London). It was a long-time resident of Fleetwood shed (13 years) and was finally withdrawn in December 1966. Rescued from Barry, it went to the K&WVR where restoration work started, but moved to Buckley Wells for completion to working order. Since entering service the locomotive has been much in demand by enthusiasts for photographic specials. Looking very smart in its BR lined black livery, it is shown crossing the River Irwell near Ewood Bridge on 25 February 1994 on one of these photographic specials. *David Dyson*

Left: Out of the 842 Stanier Class 5s No 44767 was unique. It was built at Crewe in 1947 with outside Stephenson link motion together with double chimney and Timken roller bearings. The double chimney and blastpipe, together with electric lighting, were removed during its operational career. It spent several years allocated to Bank Hall shed at Liverpool and much of its time working trans-Pennine expresses on the Calder Valley route. It was transferred to Carlisle Kingmoor for its last years and was frequently seen on freight duties over the Settle-Carlisle line. Withdrawn from Kingmoor in December 1967, it remained in store there until July 1969. It then spent many years on the North Yorkshire Moors Railway, from where it ventured out on main line specials painted in the LMS plain black livery with lined straw numerals. As can be seen, it is currently in BR lined black and is pictured near Irwell Vale on 8 October 1995. It has covered many miles on the main line recently, as well as visiting several preserved lines. *Mike Taylor*

Left: Ex-GWR 2-8-0T No 5224 visited the railway during the winter of 1992/93 and its days in steam seemed to coincide with some sunny weather. Brief details about the locomotive appear on page 19. It is based on the Great Central Railway, where it has put in many miles of service. It is seen at Ewood Bridge on a crisp winter's day about to tackle the final climb of 1 in 150 to Rawtenstall. *David Dyson*

Above: Class 45 No D61 entered service in March 1962 based at Derby and settled down to many years of service primarily working the Midland main line. Whilst allocated to Tinsley depot in its later years it was frequently seen on trans-Pennine duties until it was finally withdrawn in March 1987. It was named *The Royal Ordnance Corps* in September 1965 and renumbered 45112 in August 1973. It was dumped at March depot before being rescued by Harry Needle who transferred it to the ELR. The diesel gala week in June 1995 saw it enter service, running its first train on the 12th of the month. Its inaugural run is seen here passing Ewood Bridge on its return working to Bury. *Author*

Right: The arrival of 'Deltic' No D9019 *Royal Highland Fusilier* for the week's diesel gala in June 1995 for a 12-month period was what many enthusiasts had been hoping for for some time. It has been in regular service since its arrival and the Deltic Preservation Group has accepted an invitation to keep the locomotive at Bury for an extended stay. It is to be joined at the railway by National Railway Museum 'Deltic' No 55002 *The King's Own Yorkshire Light Infantry.* The group also owns No 55009 *Alycidon*, which is currently having a major overhaul, and No 55015 *Tulyar*, which is based at Butterley.

Entering traffic in December 1961 from Vulcan Foundry, No D9019 was based at Haymarket for its entire career, except for a short period at York before withdrawal in December 1981. It is shown passing Ewood Bridge in dramatic lighting on 25 November 1995 whilst returning to Bury. *Author*

Left: Over the years the railway has been very successful in attracting visiting engines to its galas and for longer periods on loan. This applies equally to steam and diesel locomotives.

One of the first visitors to a diesel gala was the K&WVR's Class 20 No 20031, which came for just a few days in June 1992. It is seen working nose-end first towards Bury between Rawtenstall and Irwell Vale. When built in January 1960 the locomotive was allocated to Keith in Scotland and, like many members of the class, it put in around 30 years of service with BR before being withdrawn from Toton in September 1990. *Author*

Above: Hunslet 0-6-0T No 193 *Shropshire* is making steady progress towards Ramsbottom near Townsend Fold on 5 May 1991. This was shortly after this section of line had been reopened in April and the rake of 'blood & custard' coaches was newly formed. Built in 1953 for the Ministry of Defence, No 193 saw little service initially, but was based on the Shropshire & Montgomery Light Railway in 1955 and on the Severn Valley by 1971. It then passed to Peak Rail and to the Llangollen before arriving at Bury in 1989. It is currently at Appleby-Frodingham, Scunthorpe. *Mike Taylor*

Above: 'Jubilee' No 5593 was built by the North British Locomotive Co at its Queens Park Works in December 1934. It spent most of its operational career on the West Coast main line, but around 1965 it was transferred to Leeds Holbeck, where it continued in use, mainly over the Settle-Carlisle line, until steam finished in the area in September 1967. It then passed straight into preservation at the Birmingham Railway Museum. It was restored to main line condition and repainted in LMS red. Since its main line certificate expired it has visited several preserved lines, frequently having its livery changed. So far it has appeared in LMS red, BR green, BR black and, as shown here, disguised as No 5552 *Silver Jubilee*. It is seen near Townsend Fold on 19 August 1994.
Tom Heavyside

Right: Originally built in 1956, this two-car unit was converted to battery power at Cowlairs Works in 1958 for use on the Aberdeen-Ballater line, which closed in 1966 despite its proximity to Balmoral; the last royal train over the line operated in 1965. It eventually ended up at the Derby Research Centre, being painted in the livery illustrated here. This shot was taken on 7 June 1992 at Townsend Fold when the unit was in operation during a diesel gala.

The unit was numbered Sc79998 and Sc79999, becoming known as *Gemini* when based at Derby. It has performed well on the ELR and is currently being painted into its original green livery. Modifications are also being made that will improve its performance. The unit's total weight is 70 tons (37.5 for the power car and 32.5 for the trailer) of which the batteries make up no less than 16 tons (including 2.5 tons of dilute sulphuric acid!). The unit produces 200hp and is owned by the West Yorkshire Transport Museum (Transperience) in Bradford. *Author*

Above: Sporting the 'Royal Scot' headboard, the Class 40 Preservation Society's No D335 is pictured just north of Townsend Fold during the diesel gala on 7 June 1992. As can be seen, it was running without a yellow warning panel; this has now been added and the BR TOPS number 40135 applied. No D335 was new to Crewe depot in March 1961 from Vulcan Foundry and it took up main line duties on the West Coast route. It remained allocated to this area of BR until withdrawn from departmental stock as No 97406. It passed into preservation in September 1988, arriving at Bury towards the end of that year. Since then it has been a regular performer over the line. *Author*

Above: When new in May 1961 No D345, along with Nos D346-D348, was allocated to Leeds Neville Hill and was regularly used on all East Coast main line services, in particular the 'Queen of Scots' Pullman to the north and south of Leeds. It had a minor accident in April 1983 which resulted in its withdrawal in the September of that year. It arrived at Bury in February 1984.

Prior to its overhaul, the Class 40 Preservation Group decided to paint the locomotive in the BR 'large logo' style and renumbered it 40445. Also included was the scottie dog symbol associated with Glasgow Eastfield depot. This, of course, was the livery adopted by the Class 37/4s after refurbishment; Eastfield had half of the sub-class. Many considered that the locomotive looked impressive in this livery and it was a source of regret that the class had been withdrawn prior to the introduction of the livery on BR. The locomotive is now painted in the correct BR plain blue livery. Such was the standard of the restoration, that the group was awarded the prize for the best presented preserved locomotive at the Crewe diesel gala in 1995 — a considerable triumph considering more than 100 locomotives from BR and preservation were present. *Author*

Above: 'Jinty' 0-6-0T No 7298 is owned by Derek Foster. It is one of 20 members of the 422-strong class to be preserved. New in 1924, it was withdrawn in 1966 and sent to Barry. In 1983 it was acquired from the scrapyard and restored over a five-year period. It went to the Llangollen Railway, then visited the ELR during 1988 and 1989 and became the first ex-BR main line locomotive to operate a service train on the line. In this view, taken on 22 June 1993, Townsend Fold signalbox can be seen in the background as No 7298 passes with the 17.00 from Bury. *Mike Taylor*

Right: The line is fortunate in having a very wide variety of diesel classes. This includes Class 35 'Hymek' diesel-hydraulic No D7076. As with all the other Western Region hydraulics, this locomotive had a relatively short working life, only managing to put in 10 years of service between delivery from Beyer-Peacock in May 1963 and withdrawal in May 1973. Ultimately, it finished up in departmental stock and arrived on the ELR in the early 1980s. It is shown approaching the level crossing at Rawtenstall during the diesel gala on 6 June 1992. *Author*

Far right:
Class 40 No D335, again with the 'Royal Scot' headboard, departs from Rawtenstall with a train for Bury on 7 June 1992. The Clayton train heating boiler has now been restored to use. *Author*

55

Left: The superb new station building at Rawtenstall came into use on 16 April 1992, about a year after services returned to the town. Preserved Class 121 single-unit No 55032 is shown at the station ready to leave with the 18.30 service to Bury during the summer diesel gala on 15 June 1995. These units were introduced in 1960 and were built by Pressed Steel with 300hp AEC or Leyland engines. *Tom Heavyside*

Above: A most unusual visitor to Buckley Wells in November 1995 was the replica of Robert Stephenson's *Planet*, which was built by the Friends of the Museum of Science & Industry at Liverpool Road, Manchester. The original was built in 1830 and achieved the amazing feat of hauling a train between Liverpool and Manchester in 58min for the 32 miles. There were around 40 of the type built for the Liverpool & Manchester Railway. The Planet project was launched in 1986 and the first static steam test took place in May 1992. Some £90,000 later the formal launch took place on 2 October 1992. The replica visited the ELR in order to assess its haulage capacity. *Tom Heavyside*

Above: Paddy Smith's Stanier Class 5 No 5407 has become a familiar sight on the railway during the last few years. It is shown here shunting wagons at Buckley Wells prior to working a special demonstration freight. No 5407 was one of the second batch constructed by Armstrong Whitworth in 1937. It lasted until the end of steam on BR in 1968, at which time it was allocated to Lostock Hall. Restored at Steamtown, Carnforth, and painted in lined black livery, it ran numerous main line specials in the 1970s. For a brief period around 1970 it was painted in Furness Railway red, and looked very odd. By 1980 it was back to its present fine livery and became a regular performer on the main line again, including the Fort William-Mallaig services over the West Highland line.
David Dyson

Right: There have been many more locomotives that have run on the line than is possible to illustrate in a book of this size. This picture shows a line-up outside Buckley Wells shed. Amongst those present are Stanier '8F' No 48151 (normally based at Steamtown, Carnforth), 'Jubilee' No 45596 *Bahamas* (from the K&WVR) and Standard Class 4MT No 76079 (recently named *Trevor T. Jones*). It arrived at Bury in August 1989 and remained until its transfer to the Llangollen in 1993. *Brian Dobbs*

Left: The ELR cannot be accused of not catering for every type of taste as far as locomotives are concerned: steam locomotives from this little North Eastern 'H' class 0-4-0T to No 71000 *Duke of Gloucester*, and diesels from shunters to 'Deltics'.
No 1310 shown here shunting at Buckley Wells is the oldest locomotive based on the Middleton Railway, Leeds, and was constructed in 1891 at the North Eastern Railway's Gateshead Works. A total of 24 were built over the long period from 1888 to 1923, mainly for dock shunting duties, although at the Grouping in 1923, 19 were used at Darlington North Road Works. No 1310 was withdrawn in 1931 and sold to Pelaw Main Colliery. It became the property of the National Coal Board in 1947 and went to the Bowes Railway where it worked Ravensworth Ann Colliery. When Watergate Colliery on the Tanfield branch closed in 1964 the locomotive was due to be scrapped, but was rescued by the Steam Power Trust for the sum of £300. It arrived on the Middleton Railway in June 1965 and is now in full working order. It visited the ELR in June 1993. *David Dyson*

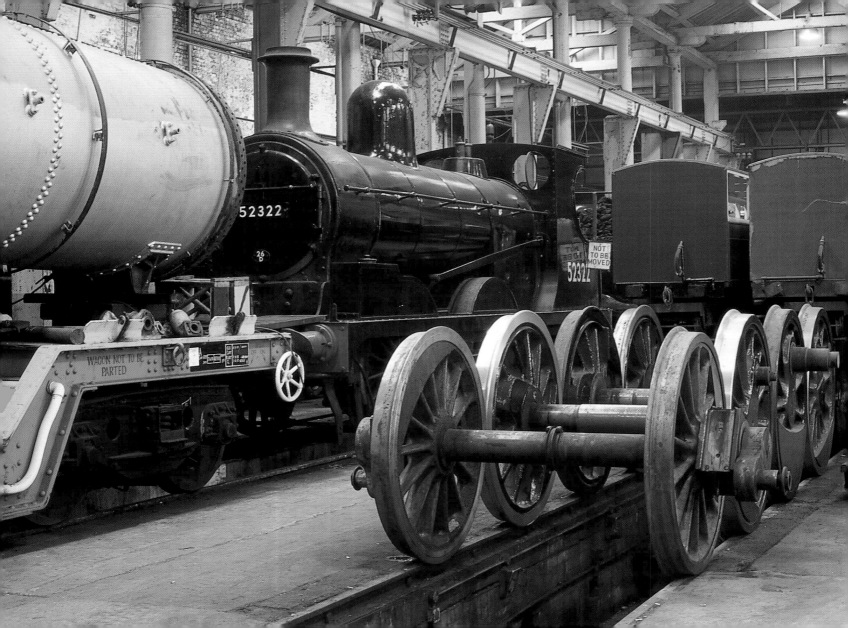

Left: No 7229, a GWR 2-8-2T, was rescued from Barry in 1985 and moved to the Plym Valley Railway in Devon. Little progress was made there and it moved to the ELR at Easter 1990. Constructed as a 2-8-0T, it never entered service in that condition, but was rebuilt as a 2-8-2T. As can be seen in this photograph taken inside Buckley Wells Works in February 1996, work is now progressing well, although no completion date has yet been set. It will be fitted with air brakes, which will no doubt upset the purists but will make it more useful to the railway. 'Jubilee' *Leander* is in the background. *Author*

Left: The ex-Lancashire & Yorkshire 'A' class stands inside the shed at Buckley Wells surrounded by rolling stock from the narrow gauge line at Steamtown, Carnforth. *Author*

Right: A view taken inside the works/shed at Buckley Wells during February 1996 shows ex-Manchester Ship Canal Hudswell-Clarke 0-6-0T No 32 in its 'Thomas the Tank Engine' blue livery. This has made it one of the best-known and most widely travelled locomotives on the line. It is looking extremely well cleaned prior to its departure to the National Railway Museum at York where it will feature as part of the celebrations for the 50th anniversary of the original books. *Author*

Right: 'Warship' Class 42 diesel-hydraulic No 832 *Onslaught* is seen on the Heywood extension in its very smart (but now removed) black livery. At the other end of the train is Stanier Class 5 No 5407. The picture was taken near Bury on 26 September 1993. The first locomotive to arrive at the station via the Heywood extension was No 71000 *Duke of Gloucester* in February 1994. The first diesel locomotive was 'Warship' No 821 *Greyhound*. *Onslaught* has been on the railway for many years, arriving on 11 February 1981 together with Class 52 *Western Prince*. *Mike Taylor*

Above: A view taken outside the EMU shed at Buckley Wells on 27 August 1982 showing some of the Class 504 units that worked the Manchester-Bury service. *Author*

Right: The track around Bury Knowsley Street was removed *c*1987 and the cutting filled in just as the trains were starting to run to Ramsbottom again. Whilst the Bury-Manchester line was closed for rebuilding into the new Metrolink system, the opportunity was taken to build a bridge over it so that the Heywood extension could be created and thus the ELR could retain a connection to the railway network. This involved digging out the cutting, with the earth being used to build an embankment on the Heywood side. Work started in 1991 and the first train crossed the bridge on 22 May 1993. Due to bridges crossing the cutting, it has been necessary to use a gradient of 1 in 29 for a short distance to gain clearance over Metrolink. Following this there is a 1 in 85 gradient for 2½ miles to Broadfield, which should produce some fine action from the steam engines when regular services start. The picture shows the newly completed trackbed on 25 March 1993.
Tom Heavyside

Right: It was very fortunate that two of the 11 handsome Somerset & Dorset 2-8-0s finished up at Woodham Bros' scrapyard in Barry. No 53809, built in 1925 by Robert Stephenson & Co Ltd, started life as S&D No 89, becoming LMSR No 9679 in 1930 and then No 13809 in 1932. Withdrawn in June 1964, just about two years before the S&D closed, it was sent to Barry from where it was rescued by Frank Beaumont, eventually arriving at the Midland Railway Centre, Butterley. It has travelled extensively on the main line and has visited a wide variety of locations, things that the class never did in BR ownership, being built for one route and never being transferred from Bath shed. The locomotive arrived on the ELR for a four-month visit in August 1993. This superb silhouette picture of the locomotive shows its elegant outline to advantage. It is crossing the River Irwell just before Burrs as it heads up the valley towards Ramsbottom. *David Dyson*